Discovering THE LIZARD

MICHAEL WILLIAMS

BOSSINEY BOOKS

First published in 1997
by Bossiney Books, St Teath, Bodmin, Cornwall

ISBN: 1 899383 08 5

Printed by Penwell Ltd of Callington

FRONT COVER PHOTOGRAPH: Ray Bishop
FRONT COVER DESIGN: Maggie Ginger
MODERN PHOTOGRAPHS: Ray Bishop
MAP: Felicity Young

Acknowledgements

Once more I am indebted to Sally Dodd for her typesetting and thoughtful
encouragement, Angela Larcombe for her editing, Maggie Ginger for her cover
design and Evan Jones of Penwell for his help in getting this title into profes-
sional shape. This then is very much a Bossiney team effort. My thanks also to
writers who have kindly allowed me to use the occasional quote, notably the
family of J.C. Trewin, an eminent son of the peninsula, for permission to use
some of his Lizard memories. Last but far from least we are grateful to Felicity
Young for her map – and Colin Benford of the Bonython Bookshop, Truro who
has read the manuscript.

DISCOVERING THE LIZARD

The Lizard peninsula is very nearly an island within an island. It is almost surrounded by water and as for Cornwall herself, but for a couple of miles or so of land around Morwenstow, she would be a complete island.

The Lizard peninsula is unique. No other part of ancient Kernow remotely resembles it. This is the land of serpentine: beautiful stones ranging from greenish black to a delicate pale turquoise, it is a vibrant stone symbolizing the region. I have long believed Cornwall is as much a feeling as a place – and each region generates a different response. Lizard reflects that belief, reflects it vividly. Lizard is the heel of Cornwall. Land's End is the Cornish toe and Mount's Bay its sole.

Some say there is no such thing as 'bad weather' on The Lizard, only 'different weather.' That eminent son of the peninsula JC Trewin writing a letter to a friend reflected: 'There were a few wet days, days at the tail of

the holiday when one understood better the Briton's need for Capri and the Bay of Naples. But, personally, I like the sea-mists. When they "lap and cling" and the foghorn moos out over the Stags, I feel withdrawn from the world, hidden in the fog. The Lizard, remote even to this day – thank goodness the railway has not struck out across Goonhilly – is never more remote than when it hangs between earth and heaven in a white tissue of vapour.'

But there are glorious Lizard days – days when you understand why it is such a popular part of Cornwall, understand too why painters and photographers are drawn like magnets. The rocky coves, the splendour of the cliffs and the everchanging seas – these are only some of the facets of the coastline. Lizard is quite simply a great edge-of-the-ocean experience.

Lizard's attractions – and claims to fame – are various. Its coastline is surely some of the finest in Britain. This is an ancient landscape with the graves of chieftains from long ago scattered about the place. The Lizard in many areas is so flat: the result of lying beneath the sea for millions of years. There are echoes of the past. The old folk could tell you where the wild goonhillies – ponies – once grazed or point to the place on the downs where highwaymen were hanged. An enigma too: the land of Saints and smugglers, of wrecks and heroic rescues, of modern communication and ghosts.

One visiting writer penned: '... the coasts here swarm with smugglers from Land's End to the Lizard ...' Folklore has it that when a 'run' was being made, a lookout was strategically placed on a certain church tower enabling him to observe the approach road and the seashore. One Lizard rector was accused of neglecting his spiritual duties because he was too busy with his other calling: that of 'free trader.' Cornish smuggling was at its high noon in the eighteenth century when high taxes made it a lucrative business – and all levels of Lizard society were involved.

Past and present easily merge and sometimes it is difficult to disentangle fact from legend. Can there be smoke without fire? Did the author of *Alice in Wonderland* find inspiration here? What made Group Captain Leonard Cheshire VC, DSO, DFC open one of his first homes for the chronic sick at Predannack? I never approach Lizard Town without thinking of my two meetings with that incredible man who became a double legend in half a lifetime: legendary airman with Bomber Command and later the Christian missionary working for people all over the world.

There is a magical atmosphere – for many of us Lizard is a never-ending love-affair. It can be all things to men and women who value contrasting beauty. Within these 48 pages I have only been able to write about *some* of the lovely places. Explore them and enjoy them.

Before we begin our exploring we had better look at the name. Jean Stubbs in her very good book *100 Years Around The Lizard* published by

Bossiney back in 1985 and now out of print, delved into the matter:

'The Lizard's old name was *Meneage*, meaning 'a monastic land'. As S.H. Burton said "The Saints have set their seal on it." So where does its newer name come from? *Lazer* the leper? There is a leper's window in Landewednack Church. A view from the sea when the promontory looks like a lizard sunning itself?

'No, *Lis-arth* means the high court or fortress. Aptly named, for this southernmost point of the British Isles stands majestically above its guardian rocks. At once secretive and intimate, sunlit and brooding, it has a thousand changes of mood and light.'

Looking towards the Lizard.

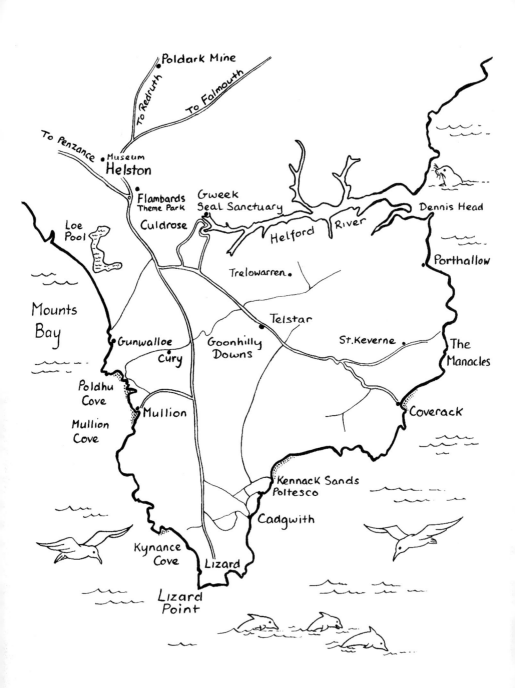

Poldark Mine

To Redruth

To Falmouth

To Penzance

Museum
Helston

Flambards
Theme Park

Culdrose

Gweek
Seal Sanctuary

Dennis Head

Helford River

Loe
Pool

Porthallow

Trelowarren

Mounts
Bay

Telstar

St. Keverne

The
Manacles

Gunwalloe

Goonhilly
Downs

Cury

Poldhu
Cove

Mullion

Coverack

Mullion
Cove

Kennack Sands
Poltesco

Cadgwith

Kynance
Cove

Lizard

Lizard
Point

HELFORD RIVER and FRENCHMAN'S CREEK

Rivers have a special quality. With timeless charm and distinct person-
ality, they add vitality to the landscape through which they flow.

In Cornwall, the Helford is one of our most beautiful and Frenchman's
Creek remains one of the most magical of its tidal branches. The very
name quickens our imagination; though locally it has been called
Frenchman's Pill or, quite simply, Pill, the Cornish word for creek.

I recall that fine travel writer, Lady Clara Vyvyan, telling me how she
found rowing up Frenchman's Creek on a rising tide 'one of the most wonderful of Cornish experiences.'

In her book on the river, she wrote: 'The first time I rowed up to the end,
or rather to the beginning of the creek, was on a day of September. I
remember looking up through the trees and seeing a glint of gold from

A LYRICAL shot of Helford captured by the camera of Ray Bishop.

AN OLD picture postcard showing the Ferry Boat Inn at Helford Passage – note the neatly laid tables outside the inn. It was obviously summer time and during a spell of good weather. Originally a passage house – the name given to establishments where people could stop for a drink while waiting for the ferry to take them across the water. Formerly known as Passage Inn, it faces the water at Helford Passage, between Mawnan Smith and Constantine. The actor David Niven spent a 'belated honeymoon' here in 1945 and shortly before his death wrote of his memory of standing in the river at Helford Passage receiving oysters from a passing boatman.

fields where the corn stood in shocks, and as I rowed on and on the line of water narrowed and the trees behind closed in on me, keeping me safe in a place where no trouble could enter, where the ancient Gods were surely reigning in serenity.'

The Helford River by C.C. Vyvyan is one of the most evocative books ever written about anywhere in Cornwall.

As for Frenchman's Creek it has been immortalised by Daphne du Maurier's novel of that name.

She and her husband sailed in their boat for the open sea after their wedding at Lanteglos Church, near Fowey, heading downchannel for the

Helford and Frenchman's Creek. 'We couldn't have chosen anything more beautiful,' Dame Daphne reflected 45 years later.

Frenchman's Creek, first published by Victor Gollancz back in 1941, has remained a bestseller for more than five decades. A mixture of romance and adventure, containing some vivid descriptions of the Helford and Cornwall in times past, it is Dame Daphne at her most beguiling as a storyteller.

While the Cornish gentry endeavour to capture the daring Frenchman who plunders our shores, the beautiful Lady Dona finds excitement, danger and passion all interwoven as she dares to love a pirate. 'A heroine,' wrote a rather pompous *Sunday Times* reviewer, 'who is bound to make thousands of friends in spite of her somewhat questionable behaviour.'

When the film *Frenchman's Creek* was made the music used on the sound track was Claire de Lune, and Joan Fontaine starred as Donna St Columb. Because it was made during the war the film makers went to North California – a sad but necessary fact.

Some years ago I did some work on the river for a radio series about Daphne du Maurier and her Cornish locations. It was a memorable experience yet curiously, for all its beauty and literary and film fame, Frenchman's Creek remains a secret place.

Perhaps not surprisingly the creek has a haunted reputation. One night an old man took a short cut across the creek. He had been drinking and probably he had the tide wrong. Anyway he did not return that night.

Next morning when the tide had receded, they found him sitting upright in the water, hat still on his head and his long white beard running with water.

Local people say his ghost has appeared in neighbouring cottages and houses that he knew in his lifetime on and along the Helford. He seems reluctant to leave. And who can blame him?

TRELOWARREN

The owners of the great houses of Cornwall were people of vision. They improved and expanded their properties. Outside and beyond that many of them were public-spirited who, given the opportunity, became MPs and High Sheriffs.

Trelowarren is the great house of the peninsula, home of the Royalist Vyvyans. Here is how Sir John Betjeman saw it in his *Cornwall, Shell Guide*, first published in 1933 and updated in 1964: 'The boundaries of their lands are marked by Gothic lodges giving on to tree-shaded drives ... glimpses of pasture and vistas of Helford river ... This is a long and two-storey building with projecting wings, substantially sixteenth century and looking over a spreading lawn.' In 1750 the Vyvyan of that period added battlements and renewed the chapel in a delightful Strawberry Hill Gothic style. Romantic is the word.

I knew it in the days when Lady Clara Vyvyan lived here. Clara Vyvyan loved growing things from childhood days and was an indefatigable walker. At the age of forty-one she and another lady plus two Indian guides crossed the great divide from Canada into Alaska, and later she walked down the Rhone river valley, from glacier source to Mediterranean delta: a walk of some four hundred miles.

Her *Letters from A Cornish Garden* – from Trelowarren of course – is a beautiful book full of perception and wisdom. Dame Daphne du Maurier in her foreword said of her friend and fellow author: 'She possesses an uncanny insight into the very nature of all things growing and all things wild.'

Not for nothing did Dr A.L. Rowse call her 'one of our best travel writers.' Her gift was such that we the reader, travelling from page to page, get the feeling that we are making the journeys too.

Sir Ferrers Vyvyan, who inherited Trelowarren from his late father, says 'The area around the Helford River owes an enormous debt to Clara and her husband Sir Courtenay. They both resisted all money offers ... people wanting to build on the banks of the Helford .. and they preserved the area at great personal financial loss. They were real pioneering conservationists.'

In 1973 Clara Vyvyan generously contributed a chapter on The Lizard for our first major Bossiney title. In it she showed how her eyes and ears captured the subtleties of Lizard life: 'One of the strongholds of dialect was the single-plank bench fixed against a wall in Cadgwith and in continual use in the good years of the fishing business. It was always sacred to the elder fisherman, for it overlooked the little beach of the little cove, also the arrival and departure of boats, the ebbing and the flowing of the tides and a V-shaped vista of the open sea. The old men used to settle there like the snails in a wall, or elders in council, while they exchanged news and memories and forecasts of the weather and criticism of the Government.

'It was the local parson who introduced me to those veterans on a day when he had taken me out mackerel fishing in his boat. He was a man as notable for his prowess among the life-boat crew as for his commendable brevity in the pulpit. His "star turn" sermon lasted exactly three minutes.

'After that introduction, I always felt that I had friends in Cadgwith, and to listen to those old sea-dogs talking in broad Cornish was like listening to music.'

The Vyvyan family, who settled at Trelowarren in 1427 and still live here have developed it and the grounds into an attractive and unspoilt estate: incredible to relate there is neither admission charge nor parking fee – and you are free to wander. Sir Ferrers Vyvyan says 'Apart from welcoming visitors to Cornwall we are relinking Trelowarren with the local Lizard community.'

Trelowarren is open from April until October when the house and Strawberry Hill Chapel, beautifully restored, are open for guided tours. Big changes have been achieved at Trelowarren but older members of the family – if they were to come back – would be pleased to see that it remains in loving caring Vyvyan hands. Moreover the new facilities, in a way, have made Trelowarren more attractive to visitors and, at the same time, providing a platform for Cornish creativity. There is a permanent exhibition centre of the Cornwall Crafts Association open until Christmas in the old stable block and outdoor theatre takes place in the grounds. A nursery garden, a pottery, a weaving workshop and bistro are all here and the Lizard Countryside Centre which displays many aspects of the peninsula including a magnificent collection of minerals found on and around the Lizard – an ideal introduction to any Lizard exploration.

Trelowarren is not just the great house of the peninsula, it is one of the most romantic and enlightened of estates.

Lady Clara Vyvyan

11

THE NATIONAL SEAL SANCTUARY AT GWEEK

The seal sanctuary, set in the beautiful Helford Estuary, acts as a rescue centre for injured and orphaned seal pups ultimately returning them to the wild. In addition the sanctuary is the home for a lively community of adult seals and sea lions.

It first opened its doors in 1957 before moving to this present location at Gweek in 1976. The pups are rescued from near certain death, and generally seal pups can be seen being cared for in the fully equipped hospital between the months of September and February.

In the words of the sanctuary's brochure:

'The fascinating story of seal rescue and release begins in our audio visual and interpretation area, and continues throughout our seal hospital, where much of the valuable rehabilitation work takes place.

'This specially equipped facility is staffed by a dedicated team of experts, who provide round the clock care and attention to the many sick and injured seal pups which arrive every year.

'Once on the road to recovery, the young pups are moved to our outdoor nursery and convalescence pools where they will gain further body weight as well as learning the skills necessary to ensure their survival when they are finally returned home to the sea.'

GWEEK. It lies quietly at the limit of the tidal flow of the majestic Helford River: one of Cornwall's almost forgotten ports.

HELSTON FOLK MUSEUM

Helston is the gateway to the Lizard peninsula, and a visit to the Helston Folk Museum in the Old Butter Market is a really worthwhile experience.

The emphasis of the museum is on crafts and industries which flourished in the nineteenth century and the early years of this century. An outstanding feature is the kitchen reflecting life styles of earlier Cornish generations, other exhibits include saddlery and wheelwright workshops, a waggonette used by the local gentry, a cider press and cider mill – both about 250 years old – and a wide range of farming tools and machinery.

Naturally there is a section relating to Helston's great date in the calendar: the famous Furry Day. It shows photographs from the turn of the century of the dances and Hal-an-Tow. A clock depicting the dancers and playing the famous tune can be heard by inserting a modest 5p coin: wonderful value for money.

There is much to see and enjoy here, and Church Street itself is one of the loveliest in Cornwall. The Market House, built in the 1830s, comprised two buildings, one selling butter and eggs and the other meat. The Museum, which opened in 1949, originally occupied the former area but has grown to such an extent that it became necessary to incorporate the meat market. It is open daily from 10.30 to 1.00 and 2.00 till 4.30, except Wednesdays when it closes at noon.

GUNWALLOE CHURCH and COVE

Gunwalloe Church *and* Cove are jewels in the crown that is Lizard. In my experience no other Cornish church *quite* generates such an atmosphere and the cove has a matching quality. In their different ways they send us on our journey renewed and refreshed. They almost bring us to our knees at first sight.

'The glory of a building,' wrote Ruskin, 'is in its age, and in that deep sense of voicefulness, of stern watching, of mysterious sympathy, nay, even of approval or condemnation which we feel in walls that have been washed by waves of humanity.' Ruskin might have been writing of Gunwalloe, and as for the waves from the sea, they wash its walls and the biggest fly over the roof.

More than twenty years ago I interviewed Frederick William Marshall who was the vicar here and at Cury: an illuminating meeting.

'I go down to Gunwalloe almost every day.' the Rev Marshall explained, 'and very often I'm conscious of something deeply spiritual there. I've never seen anything, but I've many times felt surrounded by the departed. At service, when I say: "The Lord be with thy spirit," I get a response that goes beyond the number of those present. The odour of past prayer hangs about the place.

'Have you ever heard the story of the Cornish parson who called a service on the night of All Souls? Normally, he had a very regular, very faithful flock but, on this night of All Souls, not a person turned up. Later he found out why. They believed all the departed souls came to church that night. Those who had died without repenting were kept outside the churchyard gates and walls; those who had made a little amendment were allowed to go as far as the porch; and only those who had been Communicants were allowed inside. It's said to be a true story. I'm certainly conscious of the presence of others down at Gunwalloe.'

Cornwall has had more than her share of highly individual parsons. Among them was Father Sandys Wason: 'the splendid and eccentric incumbent of Cury-cum-Gunwalloe' as John Betjeman's described him – the novelist Compton Mackenzie, when first married, used to stay with him. One evening Sandys Wason was seen genuflecting when passing the stalls gangway of a London theatre. 'You're not at Mass ...' somebody said. Wason retorted sharply: 'Everything's Mass to me!'

It is said that every church has something to say, and that is certainly true

49936 GUNWALLOE COVE AND CHURCH

of Gunwalloe. If these walls could talk, they would have tales to tell.

One of the best known Lizard smugglers was Henry Cuttance of Gunwalloe. A courteous man, Henry spent the greater part of his seventy-five years smuggling or being involved in the distribution and sale of con-traband. But his greatest and proudest claim to fame was not on the many occasions he eluded the preventive services, it was when he cheated death on a wild stormy night rescuing Norwegian seamen whose vessel had been driven ashore here at Gunwalloe. He and his colleagues braved the ele-ments in a ten hour rescue mission and, as a result of his heroism and lead-ership he earned an inscribed silver cup from the King of Norway. The old folk vowed several chests of treasure belonging to the notorious buccaneer Captain Avery lie buried in the nearby sandbanks.

We know too that in 1526 a treasure ship, belonging to the King of Portugal, was driven ashore in a wicked storm, when local men not only helped to rescue most of the crew but also retrieved much of the treasure – though not all. Then in 1807 a ship from South America was wrecked here. 140 of the crew were saved, but another 40 perished as they refused to leave the vessel. It was later discovered that the shipwrecked ship was loaded with plunder.

Over the years the occasional dollar coin has been recovered from the shifting sands. Now we shall never know the full extent of the wealth which lies hereabouts. So mystery cloaks this coastline.

FLAMBARDS VILLAGE THEME PARK, HELSTON

This is a major tourist attraction. Chairman Douglas Kinsford Hale says: 'We have improved, diversified and grown each year to ensure that there will always be something new for you to see and do ...'

Flambards Victorian Village began modestly in 1979 with just three rooms: a nursery, an old world kitchen and an aircraft workshop complementing the aircraft built for Yorkshire Television's popular series 'Flambards.' The rooms were so popular that Audrey Hale set about enlarging the theme and over the years has continued to design and equip.

BRITAIN in the Blitz as seen at Flambards.

White Star Liner "Suevic"
Wrecked at the Lizard on
Sunday March 17th 1907.
Photo by A.H.Hawke,
Helston.

Mr A.H. Hawke was a well-known Helston photographer who turned some of his best work into postcards. Here is his photograph of White Star liner Suevic wrecked at The Lizard on Sunday March 17th 1907.

In reality it has become more of a small town than a village with over fifty shops, trade premises and interiors.

Everywhere there is great attention to detail. Britain in the Blitz, for example, is a full scale street depicting life during the war years. It has the tummy-churning whine of the air raid warning, the Anderson shelter, the unexploded bomb and many other features – you can buy reproduction ration books and identity cards from the gift shop. Dame Vera Lynn, who opened the Blitz exhibition, was heard to murmer 'Yes, that's exactly as it was ...' On that same day Dame Vera planted a tree in the Aero Park to commemorate the fortieth anniversary of the D Day landings.

The Cornwall Aero Park is another impressive area boasting one of the largest privately owned collections of aircraft in Britain and being so close to the busy Royal Naval Air Station Culdrose you will often see naval aircraft flying above the park.

Flambards offers wonderful opportunities for children too: they can have fun on the water with bumper boats or move into another dimension with the 3D cinema, and bad weather need not deter, for there is Sea Legs Safari, an exciting undercover adventure centre where children can clamber, scramble and explore for hours.

Award winning gardens, clowns and jugglers, Punch and Judy, The Wonderful World of Gus Honeybun: Flambards has all these and a great deal more – and is open most days from Easter to the end of October.

POLDHU

When we come to Poldhu, we come to more than a small but beautiful cove, we come to the beginning of something immensely important. Arthur Mee, touring and researching for his book *Cornwall*, part of *The King's England* series, published back in the 1930s, wrote in his notebook: 'On the edge of the Lizard peninsula, looking down into one of the Channel's smallest coves, this point has found its way into history ... the first high power wireless station in the world.'

From this cove on 12 December 1901 the first faint signals were sent across the Atlantic Ocean to an excited Marconi in Newfoundland. Earlier, Marconi had conducted a successful transmission between the Needles and Sandbanks, a matter of 15 miles or so, but that success had set him thinking of greater distances, and consequently he established the Poldhu Station. He chose Poldhu for two very good reasons: it was a pretty private place and it offered an unobstructed path for radio waves across the ocean.

So Poldhu became an important place. To Poldhu came the very first news that the *Titanic* was sinking on her maiden voyage and from here a message to a liner in mid-Atlantic led to the arrest of the murderer Dr Crippen. In 1905 Poldhu provided a daily news service for ships, a service which was maintained until 1922. When Poldhu ceased to operate commercially, it continued for experimental purposes until 1934 when the old buildings were knocked down and this chunk of Lizard coastline passed into the care of the National Trust. The Marconi Monument stands here reminding us of those great pioneering days. Some years ago I had the pleasure of doing a radio broadcast from this historic spot with Rebecca Pickford, then a leading lady for BBC Radio Cornwall. Though ours was a modest contribution it was a moving experience to do that part of our series from the very cradle of radio.

As for Poldhu Cove, it remains a popular beach, dominated by the old Poldhu Hotel, now a residential home. Bathing is safe in settled weather conditions – but the sea must never be underestimated anywhere around this coastline – and shelter is available by the cliffs from that recurring curse of the seaside: the wind.

MULLION

Mullion is one of my favourite Cornish villages. I have many happy memories of Mullion Cricket Club, playing there, watching, umpiring and scoring. In the days when Clifford Casley was King, Mullion were a force to be reckoned with on the cricket field. Clifford made hundreds of runs for his club and the county team and is regarded as one of the best cricketers ever to come out of Cornwall; he was accomplished too on the football field, the tennis court and the golf course: a magnificent all-rounder.

In his *Coastline of Cornwall* Ken Duxbury reflected 'It is a grand bit of coast to walk, down to Church Cove, south of Gunwalloe, and on round to popular Mullion Cove which does, I suppose, get a bit of lee from the Island just to seaward. It needs it. In winter I have seen the sea thundering over that harbour wall as though it were bound for Mullion village itself.'

Mullion would have had its share of smuggling and smugglers. CA Johns, a man who knew and understood his Lizard, recalled his meeting with an old smuggler. 'He has since dropped his profession of smuggler and has on many occasions risked his life to save crews of shipwrecked vessels.' The old seaman told him the King's men did not always chase the smugglers with 'their utmost strength, for in those days, there were many sailors in the Navy who had served their apprenticeship to sea, practising the same lawless pursuit.' And the local vicar proceeded to tell him 'Many a smuggler was otherwise a good, quiet harmless creature enough, who probably thought that in assisting to run a cargo, he was hurting nobody.'

Mullion Church must be the most ornate church on the whole peninsula. It boasts some magnificent carved oak benches, and its North Door is sometimes referred to as 'The Devil's Door', as it was left open at baptisms to allow evil spirits escape.

Another interesting feature is the so-called Dog Door, a small entrance at the bottom of the main door. The informative church guide explains 'This is sometimes to be found in churches near extensive farm lands, notably in Wales, and was supposed to be for the convenience of sheep dogs attending service, whose staying power was not that of their masters ...'

MULLION Harbour and Mullion Island. As for Mullion Cove it is also known as Porth Mellin – in Cornish the word porth means harbour or cove and melyn means mill. There was a mill here in 1870 – or it could be a reference to the saint.

The roof is true Cornish style; the original timbers are said to have come from Goonhilly Forest. It was totally restored and rebuilt in the 1980s – and you will not find a single nail in the old oak timbers, all the joints pegged in medieval fashion.

This beautiful church is dedicated to St Mellanus who came from South Wales and later became Bishop of Aleth (St Malo) and died in 570 AD. His statue is in front of the rood screen. In the sixth century numerous missionaries travelled around the Celtic regions of Cornwall, Brittany, Wales and Ireland often preaching and baptising by local streams before churches were built. Many calendars passed between the death of St Mennanus and the building in its present form of the church.

Thatched Old Inn is one of the character hostelries of South Cornwall. It is understood the great Marconi held meetings here, and the sign outside shows the man himself.

The Rev Robert Francis Kilvert, whose celebrated diaries were later turned into a television series, came to Mullion in 1870 arriving in a wagonette drawn by a pair of greys. He stayed at the Old Inn where Mary Munday was the landlady. Kilvert described her as 'a genuine Cornish Celt and a good specimen of one – impulsive, warm-hearted, excitable, demonstrative, imaginative, eloquent.' He wrote how, as he and his companions waited in the sitting room over the stables, they heard the horses stomping underneath. The window looked out onto a waving field of wheat which grew close up to the wall of the inn.

POLURRIAN HOTEL and POLURRIAN COVE

Polurrian Hotel, set in twelve acres of landscaped gardens at the top of 300 feet cliffs, offers Edwardian elegance with all the modern comforts. It has a marvellous bonus in that sandy Polurrian Cove is privately owned by the hotel, only a five minute walk through the gardens and along the coastal path, the cove is sheltered and the bathing safe. Hotel guests are also automatically enrolled as members of the Leisure Club for the duration of their stay; facilities include a heated indoor swimming pool, sauna, whirlpool bath, squash and tennis courts and gymnasium.

When the cinema film *Never Let Me Go*, starring Clark Gable and Gene Tierney, was made in Cornwall in 1952, the 'King' – as Gable was called – and most of the film unit, stayed at the Polurrian for several weeks.

The peninsula is fortunate in having such an establishment and views from the terrace and the front bedrooms must rank among the best of any hotel in the whole of the Westcountry.

KYNANCE COVE

K ynance Cove is rated one of Cornwall's top beauty spots, and arguably one of the finest coves in all Britain.

The tidal sands – visible only at low tide – are fine and white, punctuated by a series of islands and rock formations into tiny individual beaches.

It was in 1846 that Prince Albert and the Royal children landed here, 'and by their kind condescension won for themselves golden opinions among the few of Her Majesty's loving Cornish subjects who chanced to be on the spot ...'

Names hereabouts stir our curiosity: Asparagus Island where asparagus once grew wild, the Devil's Bellows, a loud chasm of sea-spray, a cavity long ago christened The Devil's Mouth, The Parlour with its splendid window, and The Drawing Room green walled and carpeted with sand.

Murray's Guide, published back in 1859, said: 'The rocks appear as if they had been purposely grouped; and by their dark but varied colours pleasingly contrast with the light tints of the sandy beach and azure sea. The predominant colour of the serpentine is an olive green, but this is diversified by waving lines of red and purple, while many of the rocks are encrusted by the yellow lichen, or warmed by veins of steatite. The fragments into which the cliffs have been dissevered are pierced by caverns which are beautifully polished by the waves, and the beach is strewed with gorgeous pebbles.' And that is the essential spirit and character of Kynance today. Kynance is derived from the ancient Cornish language 'kenans', meaning enclosed valley.

KYNANCE Cove. The diarist Francis Kilvert on a visit recorded: "I have never seen anything like the wonderful colour of the serpentine rocks, rich, deep, warm, variegated, mottled and streaked and veined with red, green and white, huge blacks and masses of precious stone marble on every side, an enchanted cove …'

LIZARD TOWN

My first schoolboy impression was one of keen disappointment – I had expected rather more. My grandfather, whose family had links with Helston, always called it 'Lizard Town' so it was something of a letdown.

Truth is it was and remains a village. Furthermore loyal locals and those of us from outside, who love the place, admit Lizard is no beauty: a colony of buildings apparently constructed without much thought in terms of style or position. The superficial visitor may hurry away, but he is mistaken: this parish of Landewednack is full of history and legend – and unexpected beauty.

Nowhere else on the whole peninsula is the serpentine craft more evident. Over the years the craftsmen have worked away, turning stone into lighthouses, paperweights, ashtrays – even serpentine bracelets and cufflinks.

Tourism, of course, has changed the commercial character of Lizard like the rest of Cornwall. A visitor in the middle of the last century wrote: 'The collection of cottages which is dignified with the name of Lizard-town contains little worthy of note. The inhabitants are in general quiet, industrious, and orderly, gaining their livelihood by fishing, or working as day-labourers in the fields ...' That nineteenth century visitor would, of course, find big changes today; yet the essential magic of the place remains – for those who are prepared to get out and about and that means getting beyond the centre of Lizard Town.

ALL ROADS lead from Lizard Town. The Regent Cafe and Gift Shop photographed here have been run by the same family since 1956 providing marvellous value for money in its licensed family restaurant. I invariably try and time my Lizard business visits to coincide with lunchtime. Jim, who presides over the kitchen, specializes in local fish and crab, home-made pastries and cakes. Unlike many other eating places there is always Cornish cream available at The Regent. In the gift shop department you will find some excellent examples of local serpentine craft – items like electrical lighthouses and lamps – and a wide selection of books and maps. For me a visit to The Regent is like calling on old friends. I have been calling here for more than twenty years and keep returning.

LIZARD LIGHTS

All around Lizard Point are mighty seas and sharp rocks.

The Cornish historian AK Hamilton Jenkin, who lived inland at Redruth, told the tale of the old sailor who, departing this life, asked the parson to read the passage from the Scriptures, 'where they do tell about the Lezar' Lights.' Fortunately the cleric remembering verses from Genesis of the 'lesser Lights' which ruled the night, was able to tell the old man the story of their creation.

In the days before radar, this piece of coastline was a notorious grave-yard for numerous vessels. Yet locals violently opposed the positioning of a lighthouse here in the seventeenth century. The Cornish folk of those times complained that such a light would rob them of 'God's Grace' – their description of the substantial 'harvest' they reaped from shipwrecks.

Nevertheless the Lizard has the distinction of being Cornwall's senior sea light.

The man with the idea was Sir John Killigrew, whose family were noto-rious smugglers. He wanted a light for financial reasons – that he might charge dues to every vessel which sailed by in safety. The debate – for and against a lighthouse – rumbled on for years. Eventually in December 1619 a light burned here, but Killigrew ran into problems: opposition to the light persisted and he had great difficulty in collecting dues. Killigrew aban-doned the light and returned to his former way of life – a more profitable one.

Not until, 1752 was another light erected on The Lizard, a brace of coal-fired lights providing the illumination. Lights and buildings were mod-ernised in 1812 and then electrified in 1878.

There is a delightful story concerning one sleepy keeper who was employed at The Lizard during the Napoleonic wars. Slumbering at his post, he had allowed the light to burn dangerously low. The captain of a passing government packet was so angry that he ordered his gunner to fire cannon shot at the 'wished' light. No damage: but in our imagination we can picture the startled activity of one rudely awakened keeper as he fever-ishly worked to stoke up the dying fire.

At the time of writing, the lighthouse is open to the public, usually an hour after noon and an hour before dusk.

Lizard Light has come a long way since that pair of coal-fired lights. At night its flashing white patterns continue the great Lizard tradition.

LIZARD cottages photographed in 1912.

LIZARD LIGHTS depicted on an old picture postcard: Cornwall's very first light. That original light, with Eddystone off Plymouth, was intended to guide vessels entering the English Channel as well as marking their first landfall. Lizard rightly occupies an important place in British maritime history.

PISTOL MEADOW

Pistol Meadow is a curious place – for me anyway.

First, it is a haunted spot and as a member of the Ghost Club Society I have a special interest in the subject. Here, and around The Lizard in general, you feel you are often at the edge of the unknown.

Pistol Meadow is also a grim reminder: this is a beautiful but wicked coastline. Back in the 1700s, a transport ship was wrecked off the Maenheere Rocks – with horrific loss of life – there were only two survivors. The victims are buried here beneath the tamarisk bushes in mass graves.

JC Trewin once recalled: 'I can believe anything of this meadow especially after a December sunset. It was in December that I had an odd experience, about four o'clock on a calm, dull afternoon during the Armistice Autumn. In the narrows of the cliff path above Pistol, I heard someone coming, a brisk patter of feet and stood aside to let him pass. He was, as I remember, a shrivelled man in a nondescript blue guernsey, badly torn at the collar. He had a fuzz of wiry, greying hair. Nothing else was noticeable, but his eyes, deep black in the extreme pallor of his face. I said "Good afternoon." He brushed by me, without answering. A few seconds later, not more, I heard steps again, and there coming towards me, was without a doubt the same man, though manifestly he could not have doubled round in so short a time and on so awkward a path. I stopped, more perplexed than frightened, and again said "Good afternoon." Again there was no reply. And then a third time, I heard steps. Now nothing was in sight. I felt a quick stirring in the air, but no-one passed me. Fear came, and I tore home through the darkening day.'

THE LIZARD and
THE SPANISH ARMADA

Often as a young man I stood at The Lizard and tried to imagine the Spanish Armada sailing by on its way to defeat – and into history. Of course, I knew all about Sir Francis Drake and Plymouth Hoe – and *that* game of bowls. But in the eye of a Cornishman's imagination I wanted to see it from *here*: Britain's farthest south.

Imagine my delight in 1975 when JC Trewin sent me a chapter for one of our first Bossiney titles called *Both Sides of Tamar*, now long out of print but well worth tracking down in a second-hand bookshop. In it he recalled his Lizard roots and touched on that July afternoon. A distinguished author and highly respected London theatre critic Mr Trewin wrote:

'At any season the place was full of characters: my First Witch. a perfectly harmless crone from mid-village, who seemed to spend her time wrecking, combing the beaches for driftwood or any of the flotsam – varying between corks, oranges, and fountain-pen fillers – the sea might throw up between Housel and Caerthillian; a muscular, swarthy man who had a Spanish name, pronounced as spelt, and a trick of carrying on any conversation at a range of two hundred yards; and a bearded postman, with a bullseye lantern, who liked to read aloud any postcards he delivered to you. This was a child's response. The lonely ingrowing village was a community of friends.

'For any child a splendid world. At heart, I am sure, it has not changed, though too much is happening on Goonhilly Downs, the dark barrens (the "wylde moore called Gunhilly"), that we first cross on the road from Helston. The huge naval airfield of Culdrose sprawls over the site of my grandfather's farm; elsewhere, an obtrusive radio contraption must baffle anyone who thinks yet in terms of Marconi at Mullion. Once we get to it, Lizard Town is much as it used to be, especially when the visitors and their cars have pulled out and the South can lapse again into its proper peace. The South ... but we have also to recognise Compton MacKenzie's words: "The magic of the West that haunts the air from Boscay to the Hesperides is no more potent than in the Meneage, where – as in the north-west the basalt – the serpentine breaks into the granite rock as strange as the Phoenician trafficker of long ago."

'Looking back, I remember at random the churring of the serpentine-workers' wheels, lamplight on the polished stone, the faded brocade of clifftop turf, a smell of geranium, musk and seaweed, the tale of *Moyar Diu* read on Pentreath beach, the masts of the barque *Queen Margaret>* canted over in wreck. Much more: Housel pools starred with anemones, those broad double hedges on which we walked to Kynance or Cadgwith – a stranger called it "trudging on a fence" – white-tissued sea-mists ("squitchery" weather), a lane behind the church where we gathered sloes, Landewednack rookery at evening, sunsets that flowered above The Rill, and the escalading darting rush of coastline from Old Lizard across to Kynance. The names are a litany: Pentreath, Caerthillian, Pistol, Poleor, Housel, Penolver, Kilcobben, Polbream.

'Once I had the joy of presenting prizes at the village school where I went for two years. On that summer day I was able to tell young Landewednack about my personal obsession: the Spanish Armada on the Lizard sea. It sailed up from the South on a July afternoon in 1588. Watchers high on The Rill saw it coming. They heard the mutter of cannon as the Lord High Admiral of Spain; Don Alonzo de Guzman, Duke of Medina-Sidonia, had a consecrated, gold-embroidered banner run to his masthead, and every galleon in his fleet, the squadrons of Portugal and Biscay, of Castile and Andalusia, Guypuscoa and the Levant, fired a broadside:

' *"A dying fall, a fading wraith,*
A sound soon hushed again,
The Great Armada's whispered breath,
The ghostly guns of Spain."

'Rapidly, warning beacons flared along the Cornish coast. Anyone who stood that evening on Penolver would have discerned the Armada far out, vague shapes, upon each sail a great red cross; the galleons moving slowly forward in an oblique crescent, seven miles from tip to tip, "like the moon when it lies upon its back," with all the chivalry of Spain on board; Don Alonzo de Leyva, Don Diego de Valdez, Don Juan Martinez de Recalde, Don Miguel de Oquendo, Don Martin de Bretandona.'

' "There," my father would say to me when he was at home: "There boy – that's where the Dons came up from southward." And, just as I would strain to see Brazil, so I would gaze hopefully from Penolver into the dazzle of the afternoon across an empty southern sea.'

33

LANDEWEDNACK CHURCH

Some churches have a real sense of history. This church is such a shrine. On the one and only occasion I heard its bells it was worth remembering these bells of Landewednack have been ringing out for six hundred years.

There is a simplicity here, a splendour too: take a look at the tower with its contrasting blocks of pinkish granite and dark green serpentine. Landewednack is the parish of Lizard Point and here its spiritual centre. Like the majority of Celts, we Cornish often have a deep sense of religion – and you feel that quality in this lovely setting.

'The church (St Winwallo) is among elms and sycamores on a sheltered slope with old colour-washed cottages near, a change from the Lizard village above. 'That was how Sir John Betjeman, the Poet Laureate, remembered the place when he came in the early 1960s.

In Landewednack Church, the most southerly church in all Britain, the last service in Cornish was preached: the year was 1678. The present day

pulpit is made of polished chunks of serpentine, that stone which somehow symbolizes Lizard, setting it apart from the rest of Cornwall.

Out in Landewednack Churchyard, think of brave Robert Sampson, rector in the 1640s, when the plague struck. Truly a man of God, he continued to work among his people in a nightmare experience, administering the last rites, and comforting those who mourned. Inevitably he caught the plague, and lies buried with many of his people by these Cornish elms.

This parish also produced a sturdy cleric in the person of Thomas Cole who is reputed to have walked to Penryn and back, a distance of roughly twenty five miles, at the incredible age of 120, surely worth a place in *The Guinness Book of Records.*

As you go away take with you some words by another rector of Landewedack, G. Frederick Simpson:

'Pause, stranger, as you pass beneath
Where Norman art and Gothic skill
Have wrought a miracle in stone
That time has made more lovely still
Here, in this shrine, above this sea,
There breathes the faith that made you free.'

KENNACK SANDS

These twin sandy beaches are curiously underwritten. Time and again I have opened a book on Cornwall and found no mention – personally I rate Kennack Sands among the glories of the south coast.

Our celebrated novelist Dame Daphne du Maurier in her book *Vanishing Cornwall* wrote '... recovering from measles at the age of ten, and staying some three miles or so from Lizard Point, I taught myself to swim on Kennack Sands. Or, rather, in a pool set beneath the cliffs ...' In a conversation, many years later, and further up the coast near her beloved Fowey she told me: '... even then the sea seemed cruel, demanding victims.'

I am writing these words at my desk, back at St Teath in North Cornwall. Close by one of my library shelves are two pebbles from Kennack Sands. Their very presence lift the spirits.

One man who knew all about Kennack Sands was the Rev CA Johns who on his Lizard exploration back in the 1840s gives his readers this vivid word portrait: 'a narrow yellow line indicates a sandy beach, known by the name of Kennack Sands. The opposite boundary of the bay is formed by a bold, bluff, head-land. the Black-head, a most appropriate name, for the whole face of the cliff, with the exception of one narrow perpendicular strip, called Sparnick, is of a remarkable dingy hue. In the distance, the Deadman Point is distinctly visible, with a vessel or two entering or quitting Falmouth Harbour, which lies between; and if the weather be very clear, the Rame Head the most easterly head-land in the country, may be described stretching out a long way on the horizon, as unsubstantial in appearance as a fog-bank. One or two lobster catchers are creeping along under the cliffs in their tiny vessels, and few fishing boats of a larger size are making for the offing, there to set their drift-nets, as soon as night sets in; just beneath us, on a projecting ledge of rock, lie the whitening bones of a lamb, killed and devoured by ravens, before it was strong enough to seek safety by flight; and the deep croak of the same bird, or the shrill note of the jackdaw, divides with the dashing of the sea below us and its murmuring roll beyond the whole empire of sound.'

KENNACK SANDS in winter ▶

36

GOONHILLY EARTH STATION

Earth Station Goonhilly is not only the biggest operational satellite communications centre in the world, it is an opportunity personally to experience the wonders of the space age. These satellite dishes at Goonhilly have probably transmitted 'more epoch-making events than those at any other station on earth.'

Named after great characters in Cornish folklore, each of the satellite dishes has done its own bit of history. Merlin, for example, beamed Live Aid around the globe and the Gulf War was transmitted by Pellinor.

Earth Station Goonhilly is a perfect all weather outing as virtually all your visit is under cover. As the station's brochure puts it: 'Experience the world of satellite technology. Join us in our 50 seat film theatre for a fabulous journey through time and space; operate an antenna dish for yourself, scanning the skies for television signals from all over the world, or surf the Net in our Internet Zone.'

At the time of writing the station opens from early April until the end of November. It is located at Goonhilly Downs, seven miles from Helston on the B3293 St Keverne road, and Goonhilly Downs are part of the Lizard National Nature Reserve.

CADGWITH

Set at the seaward end of a delightful valley, Cadgwith is one of the gems on the whole peninsula. This tiny fishing village with its twin coves is almost too pretty to be true, and, on a brilliant summer's day it has the air of the Mediterranean.

There is a great fishing tradition, and it is appropriate to recall that the first service of the lifeboat, established at Cadgwith in the year 1867, was to rescue the local seine net, laden with fish, the loss of which would have been a bitter blow for the village. The Cadgwith lifeboat, in its time, saved as many as 522 lives: a then Cornish record which speaks volumes for native heroism and tells us something about the treachery of the seas around this Lizard coastline. Nowadays, of course, tourism has become a major plank in the economy, but Cadgwith remains a working place for

AN OLD Cadgwith postcard reflecting a quieter way of life. The children sitting in the road would now be very elderly Cadgwith residents. Scenes such as this show why Lizard Country was so popular with the early photographers.

Lizard fishermen catching crab and lobster. The two small beaches are divided by The Todden, a diminutive headland. Cadgwith has no harbour and local boats launch and retrieve from the slipway in the old style.

I remember coming here on one occasion with photographer Ray Bishop and Felicity Young, painter and book illustrator. It was a brilliant sunlit morning, and they both said how the brilliance of light can intensify everything around us. On these diamond-sharp days you can understand how and why Lizard is such popular territory for painters and photographers. The visual subjects are here by the sea, in the sky and the contrasting landscapes.

Whether you come in a car or on a cycle or on foot, you drop down into Cadgwith, white-washed cottages clinging to the steep narrow roadway and clustered around the beach where fishing boats are winched up above high tide mark. You will find holiday accommodation and, for the coastal path walker, a welcome inn.

A number of buildings are thatched, a relatively unusual sight in Cornwall where slate has dominated since the nineteenth century – some of the eaves are chained down.

Motorists are strongly advised to use the car park up the valley. One tourist, Walter White of London, back in 1854 needed no such advice. In high summer he struggled, on foot, along the cliffs to Lizard in a gale – which almost drove him headlong into a chasm nearby. The Devil's Frying Pan is a considerable crater, where the roof of a deep cave has fallen in, leaving an arch of rock with boiling seas below. Little wonder that Walter White said Cornwall appeared 'to be subjected to visitations from the Evil One.' Like Wilkie Collins, he found this area of Cornwall charged with supernatural undertones. Daphne du Maurier has said 'The time to walk about the Lizard headland is in winter or early spring ...' Then the sense of the past is often strongest.

Is this strong sense of the past why the peninsula has such a haunting and haunted air? As a member of the Ghost Club Society I have several reports of hauntings in and around this part of Cornwall.

Though a serious investigator into paranormal activity for more than thirty years, I have learnt one must keep a sense of perspective.

Late one summer evening a gentleman residing on the peninsula was walking home after a drink or two at his local inn when he became convinced that 'a supernatural something was ahead of him to the side of the lane. 'I could see this odd shape and hear strange noises,' he told me, 'and I was very nervous about passing it. But eventually I screwed up the courage to carry on walking, and when I came to this "supernatural something" it turned out to be a pig sleeping and snoring in the hedge!'

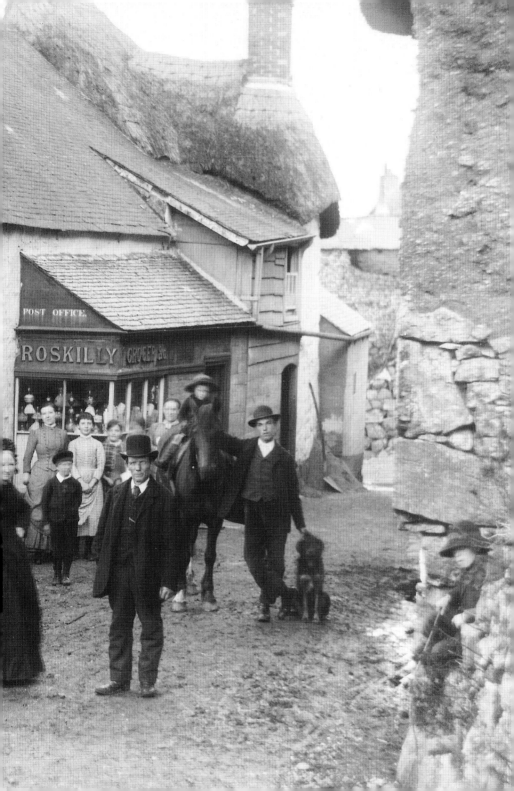

COVERACK

Coverack is its name today – but times were when it was known as Porth Coverac. The word in our ancient Cornish language means 'hideaway' and that is appropriate for a place with such a smuggling past.

Yet Coverack is an oddly underwritten location. I know three excellent books on Cornwall, all aiming to present a broad but detailed portrait of Kernow – and Coverack fails to get a sentence in any of them.

Coverack stands on the edge of serpentine country: Dolor Point and cliffs to the south – Chynalls Point with Iron Age cliff castle, the level topped Black Head and Pedn Boar – all shaped out of that beautiful rock. Then the other way – to the north – are the slopes of Coverack's own bay and beyond Dean Point and Manacle Point.

The old smugglers were laws unto themselves. In 1840 more than a hundred ankers of contraband spirits were seized – an event which put the smugglers in a curious spot because they had customers waiting. Consequently they embarked on a second episode. Advancing on the Customs House, the Lizard smugglers surprised the guards and quickly removed the kegs but not all of them. They left three kegs behind for the Customs House men.

Though Rugby is *the* game in Cornwall nowadays, Cornish wrestling has a far longer history. Nobody is sure of wrestling's genesis but historians tell us at the Battle of Agincourt, where banners depicted the different county contingents, the Cornishmen had two wrestlers on theirs. In the old days some fierce wrestling matches took place on the battery at Coverack. These matches made a deep impression on one young man. James Polkinghorne, who was born at St Keverne, went on to become one of the most celebrated Cornish wrestlers of all time. James was a huge man with the neck of a bull, dark hair, curling sideboards, piercing eyes and the most determined of jaws. His deeds have put him into the folklore of Cornish sport. James Polkinghorne died in 1845 but as long as Cornishmen 'wrastle' his name will be remembered and respected.

THE OLD post office at Coverack around 1900. Villagers pose for a visiting photographer. It is an extraordinary fact that in those seemingly leisurely days you could send a card or letter announcing your arrival at a certain destination next day, knowing the card would arrive first. The village post office too was a great place for gathering news – and gossip.

ST KEVERNE

Time and ocean have made St Keverne what it is – a tragic place in a green land which has been truly called 'The Garden of Cornwall.'

Off the coast are the Manacles, a reef almost hidden at high tide, dreaded by sailors and a menace to ships coming into Falmouth Harbour. In the olden days of sail, Falmouth Bay was busy with the coming and the going of the Falmouth Packets and all the other vessels, the military transports, ships of war and trading vessels. St Keverne churchyard has more than 400 shipwrecked victims: every one a grim reminder of the Manacles.

The spacious church, a notable landmark on this rocky coast, is well worth a visit. Windows and monuments, in their differing ways, tell us something about the sternness of the elements.

The north eastern part of the peninsula, comprising Mawgan, St Martin, Manaccan, St Anthony and St Keverne was popularly referred to as Meneage by the old Lizard folk, and that, in turn, is thought to be connected with manach, a monk, and rather suggests monkish land. Thus reasoned the Cornish scholar Charles Henderson who felt there was probably a number of small monasteries in the area. As for the Celtic Keverne he was a notable Saint and a special friend of his neighbour St Just. But they clashed badly when St Just, being entertained by St Keverne, made off with a chalice prized by his host. St Keverne chased his 'friend' across the countryside and, getting within range, hurled a stone at the fleeing St Just who, realizing the game was up, dropped the chalice. St Keverne thus recovered the chalice and one hopes the two Saints eventually settled their differences over some wine. You cannot travel far in Cornwall without being reminded of our Saints. A wit once said: 'There are more Saints in Cornwall than in Heaven!'

MICHAEL Joseph, Michael An Gof, a famous son of the peninsula, the St Keverne blacksmith and a great Cornish patriot. It was he who led a Cornish army on their march from Cornwall to London in 1497. Michael Joseph and Thomas Flamank, a Bodmin Lawyer, were executed when King Henry VII turned his troops on the rebel Cornish force at Blackheath.

ST ANTHONY-in-MENEAGE

Its lanes are like a fairyland, the walls high-hedged with green, crowned by great trees; we can come by a circling narrow lane which drops steeply down as it sees the church tower far below, or by a way that rides along, then high above, the delightful Gillan Creek.'

That was Arthur Mee recalling his visit more than sixty years ago. I paid my first visit thirty years later, and recall it as if it were yesterday morning: not a brilliant day but even in late winter St Anthony had a breathtaking beauty. Arthur Mee went away with a vivid memory: 150 candles burning from twenty candelabra hanging from the roof of the church. My abiding memory was the spirit of the place: the tranquillity and the remoteness. In the old days residents of Gillan – the hamlet opposite – going to church at St Anthony crossed the water by boat or walked at low tide.

Yes, a very remote spot yet incredibly medieval documents show Gillan shipped fish, oil and slate in local boats to Southampton.

To the east and guarding the entrance to the creek is Dennis Head – in Cornish dinas means fort – which was held by the Royalists during the Civil War. Together with St Mawes Castle it protected the flanks of Pendennis Castle, and the view from the headland confirms its strategic

value, commanding views of the Helford estuary, Falmouth Bay, Gerrans Bay and the Dodman. Dennis Head has been fortified since the Iron Age and during the Civil War was under the command of Sir Richard Vyvyan. He and his troops had twenty-six guns but, besieged by the Parliamentarians in 1646, eventually they had to surrender through lack of ammunition.

It is difficult to think of conflict in such a place and though many Cornishmen were more concerned about their livestock and their crops, the war did, in fact, cause bitter divisions – sometimes even inside the same family. But let us enjoy the healing qualities of this corner of the peninsula and especially its church dedicated to Saint Antoninus. Sir John Betjeman, who knew, loved and understood his Cornish churches, reckoned it had 'a Breton look.'

Today the little grey church remains one of the glories of Cornwall, and is looked after with loving care as Sonia and I discovered on a Saturday morning in 1996 when we met two local church ladies. Arthur Mee would be pleased to know that the beautiful candelabra remain in position.

There is an old Lizard theory that the remote and romantic situation of St Anthony is due to a band of shipwrecked Normans who were caught in a storm when crossing the Channel. They were driven ashore and vowed if they were saved they would build a church here. Far fetched? Maybe not because the tower is built of a fine grained granite, a type unknown in ancient Kernow but found in Normandy.

As for St Antoninus: pictures of the Saint usually show him with a pig – his emblem – hence the old label for people born in this parish: St Anthony Pigs. The original name of the Parish Feast, held on the Sunday nearest the 26th day of December, is Piggy Feast.

POLDARK MINE

Though not strictly on the peninsula, Poldark is sufficiently near to be included – and well worth a visit. Poldark is situated between Helston and Redruth on the B3297. A strange almost haunting atmosphere fills and the tunnels and workings; so much so you can almost feel the presence of the old miners.

Machinery exhibits from the past are positioned around the gardens and within the museum chambers. Some are in working order; others stand quiet – all vivid reminders of our Cornish heritage and the great industrial revolution.

The Cornish Heritage Collection features a reconstruction of 'The Poldark Village' depicting the living conditions of Ross and Demelza Poldark, the hero and heroine of the celebrated Poldark novels by Winston Graham which were later turned into an immensely popular television series. Winston Graham, who lived for some years at Perranporth, is one of the world's leading novelists. Apart from the Poldark series, he has written more than thirty books and his novels have been translated into seventeen languages.

MORE BOSSINEY BOOKS ...

EDGE OF THE UNKNOWN
Michael Williams
'These investigations into psychic phenomena are some of the more fascinating in more than thirty years of ghost hunting.'

LEGENDS OF CORNWALL
Sally Jones

MYSTERIES OF THE SOUTH WEST
Tamsin Thomas

GHOSTS & PHANTOMS OF THE WEST
Peter Underwood, Life President of the Ghost Club Society

SECRET CORNWALL
Introduced by Madeleine Gould of BBC Radio Cornwall

THE CORNISH WORLD OF DAPHNE du MAURIER
Contains a previously unpublished chapter by Dame Daphne

DISCOVERING BODMIN MOOR
E.V. Thompson

KING ARTHUR IN THE WEST
Felicity Young & Michael Williams

We shall be pleased to send you our catalogue giving full details of our growing list of titles and forthcoming publications. If you have difficulty in obtaining our titles, write direct to Bossiney Books, Land's End, St Teath, Bodmin, Cornwall.